Flower Arranging
for Fun

HAZEL PECKINPAUGH DUNLOP

BONANZA BOOKS • NEW YORK

ACKNOWLEDGMENTS

The author acknowledges with appreciation and gratitude the impetus given her interest in flower arrangement by Mary Averill, pioneer in Ikebana in this country, who was still working with flowers at the age of ninety. Also acknowledged are the friendly interest, generous cooperation, and objective examples given by Mrs. John S. Newberry and Mrs. Dexter M. Ferry, Jr. Remembered with obligation and affection are the genuine interest, guidance, and encouragement of the late Joseph B. Mills and Ralph R. Yonker and of Reuben Ryding during their tenures as publicity directors of the J. L. Hudson Company. The author is grateful to Bruce Collins, William Bartel, Ralph W. Peterson, and John R. Moore for their horticultural advice, and the author and Mr. David D. Dunlop acknowledge the photographic assistance, suggestions, and critical analyses given by Mr. George Kawamoto.

Copyright © 1959 by The Viking Press, Inc.
Published in 1959 by The Viking Press, Inc.
625 Madison Avenue, New York 22, N.Y.
Published in Canada by
The Macmillan Company of Canada Limited
Library of Congress catalog card number: 59-6593
Printed in the United States of America

(B)

Contents

Introduction

AFTER COMMODORE PERRY'S ARRIVAL in Yedo in 1853 and our subsequent treaty with Japan, interest in this unusual land began to grow in the Occident. That Japanese customs, products, and arts would in time become familiar to us in America was only natural. One of the arts, an important aspect of Japanese culture, has become particularly well known and appreciated on these shores. This is, of course, Ikebana, or flower arrangement.

It is now half a century since Mary Averill journeyed to Japan, became deeply impressed with the use of flowers as practiced by the Japanese, studied for years under their masters, and returned to her native land to tell about it in her books and teachings. The spark that was kindled here two decades ago has never abated.

Admittedly, in its first half-century, flower arrangement as a practiced art in America has experienced growing pains; doubtless it will experience more. Yet if at the present time it suffers frequently from too much "little-knowledge" judging at flower shows, its pathway only parallels that of other and older exhibited arts. It takes a long time before any new form of art is fully under-

Scotch pine, bronze-colored chrysanthemums, yellowed ginkgo leaves, and shaped branches of Japanese driftwood are arranged in a modern basket. The antique bronze Buddha and the scroll balance the design at the left side.

7

stood and universally accepted. Although often confronted with "rules" by those people who must lean on them, the student of flower arrangement today is more and more concerned with a study of underlying esthetic principles. This is because a basic understanding of good design always leads to freer and more creative work. In other words, while rules are made to help us, they can also prove a hindrance if they are too slavishly followed.

The serious pursuit of flower arrangement was once almost solely the province of the garden club. Indeed, it was the rare florist who did not look with humor on such rarified "goings-on." But no more. Increased numbers of our flower merchants have learned the importance of design and as a consequence naturalness and simplicity is more prevalent in their arrangements. Across the country we now find schools of art and design, horticultural and home economics groups, artists and decorators, all working with flowers in pattern. As a result, home decoration has become increasingly alive with colorful and pleasingly arranged floral materials. The general standard becomes higher each year.

For women who seek a hobby, flower arrangement is one of the most fascinating they can choose. However, in spite of views occasionally expressed to the contrary, flower arranging cannot be mastered in one afternoon by attending an easy-chair, leisurely lecture. It takes study and thought and practice, but all of this is of the most pleasurable kind.

Flower arranging offers a challenge. The exploration of its full possibilities provides exercise for the imagination and an intriguing intimacy with plant life as well. Many who little thought their nail polish might ever be subjected to such mutilation have become wonderful dirt gardeners as their happy acquaintance with flower arrangement grew.

CHAPTER ONE

Selection of Materials

TO PAINT A PICTURE one must have tubes of paint, a palette, brushes, canvas, and an idea. Naturally, if it is to be a satisfactory picture and please its viewers, a measure of skill and the ability to formulate an idea are also requirements in its creation. It is just as possible to produce skillful pictures with floral media. The originator must, however, have adequate physical props as well as an awareness of fitness and of beauty. One of flower arranging's early lessons should be "the art of observing." The only prerequisite is the *desire* to see, without which an intelligent selection of suitable materials to combine in an arrangement is not consistently possible.

The human race is prone to feel that the grass across the fence grows greener, so searching for plants which are rare and exotic at the local level is a typical urge all of us understand, and perhaps are inclined to let ourselves overdo. Not long ago, while I was attending a New York City Symposium, another visitor remarked to me, "Don't you have the feeling everyone is trying too hard to impress with great quantity or with rarity, thus too often reaching beyond beauty?" Her point was well taken. True enough, flowers are appropriately forced months before their normal blooming season, while still others are shipped in ahead of local blossom time and the florist adds to his stock with plants unfamiliar to the locale. But although rare florists' material is useful in winter months, it is certainly not necessary to rely on it at other times. There is just as much beauty to be discovered in local materials, in common flowers that are plentiful in season and cost little.

Nature has her lavish seasonal outpourings, and recompense is due her in floral design. Mrs. J. O. Martin of Atlanta, Georgia, tells of her visits to European flower markets where goldenrod is cultivated as a flower and commands a fair price. Yet one sure way to court elimination in many an American flower show would be through its usage. Since the goldenrod, according to latest findings, is not the universal culprit which causes hay fever suffering, an honest evaluation would disclose "commonness" as the provocation for often ignoring it.

All around us nature is constantly contriving curves with rightfully straight branches. Some atmospheric condition may change the normal coloring of a leaf or bud. Pollination may provide some different form, or bugs contribute an interesting distortion. Looking for such material and recognizing its interesting character and the possibilities of its use in an arrangement can be a fascinating and rewarding pastime.

Gray and gray-green foliage is invaluable to an arranger. It mixes well with flowers of every color and looks lovely in monochromatic arrangements, too. Eucalyptus, with its round leaf form and gray-green coloring, does not grow in the North, but is available at florists everywhere and avidly sought-after for its unusual form and color. Yet one wonders if either its texture or coloring are more beautiful than Russian olive or mullein weed? True, the tall, flexible forms of eucalyptus are usually attractive; but the velvetlike texture of a mullein's young flower stalk will provide a lovely gray, yellow-accented, vertical line. Russian olive has dramatic curves, and no plant provides a purer, softer gray in the early spring.

Soft yellow dahlias, blue lupine, smooth green grapes, and Boston ivy contrast dramatically with the rough textures of wild dock leaves, milkweed pods, and orange-yellow cockscomb arranged in a green pottery vase.

10

Every arranger will do well to set up a month-by-month scrapbook of the best locally available materials, season by season. During the winter, in the North, special attention is usually given to the various evergreens. *Juniperus communus,* with its charming, turquoise berry, and low-growing *J. Pfitzeriana* with turquoise, brown, and purple overtones are at their best around January. As temperatures drop, the rich colorings of many evergreens are more and more apparent. Also, in the winter garden we may find the Christmas rose, followed by the February rose (actually the *Helleborus*) as well as the berried *Euonymus europaeus* or *E. radicans. Pyracantha* pods and *Mahonia* foliage belong in a January listing, for they are still usable then.

February repeats many of the January listings, and when temperatures are at thirty to forty degrees, branches can be cut from various flowering trees and shrubs such as magnolia, pear, or forsythia and brought inside for forcing. By February, hothouse rhubarb should be available from the stock of the green grocer. The value of this pink and chartreuse perennial is too often overlooked by arrangers. Stalks and leaves of rhubarb should be carefully selected for color and perfection and with some gradation of size. When a rhubarb stem is weak, its hard end should be cut off and the stem placed deep in cold water; in a short time it will be perky and usable. Any color plan utilizing rhubarb might highlight the stem with flowers of like hue, dramatize the yellow in the leaf with daffodils (shipped in or forced in February), or stress the chartreuse in the leaf by using white blossoms.

Spring arrives with March, and together they reintroduce several winter-captive shrubs and flowers. Or take a shovel in hand for a visit to the woods and look for the first skunk cabbage blossom and foliage. Dig a few roots and deposit the plants in a small can of water and the leaves will continue growing into interesting forms—without odor.

Flowers come and go in a fast, vast parade of form and color. After listing local materials, separate notes on useful and not-too-expensive florist items,

Clusia foliage surrounds a fresh-cut bamboo stalk in this sophisticated contemporary design. Green pottery parakeets perch above a bright red *Arisaema triphyllum* (jack-in-the-pulpit) seed pod. The bamboo is nailed to a board set in the bronze container.

especially foliage, can be helpful in planning what to use when and where. There are certain seasons when shipped-in materials are more plentiful, better in quality, and lower in cost. This can be noted. Then, too, at certain seasons the habitual coloring of a plant may be altered by weather. Such is the case with *Galax* leaves. These are normally green in their natural habitat, but around February and March, after frost has applied its paintbrush, they take on rich, brown tones that are useful in many an arrangement.

There are great possibilities for drama in the use of large flowers and leaves, and a knowledge of their special characteristics can be important. For instance, a branch of thornapple, when forced, can be beautiful and dramatic; but if it is cut later, when the foliage is out, the overall pattern of the branch is "busy" and not nearly so effective. A reason for selecting the calla lily is its bold, clean-cut form. Although it is no more beautiful than many smaller flowers, it can be relied upon for a dramatic arrangement. The Strelitzia, to my mind, is not one of nature's most beautiful gifts; yet, when skillfully used, it is capable of startlingly attractive results.

Without doubt, selection of material is important. After mechanics are mastered and basic formations are understood, cultivating the "art of observing" makes the pathway to successful designing a far easier road.

CHAPTER TWO

Design

To DESIGN, according to no less an authority than Webster, is "to fashion according to a plan; to conceive or execute a scheme or plan." Thus, designing with flowers must be a conscious process. To begin with, the idea of the design may be somewhat nebulous; but as the selection of material progresses and a container is chosen, the idea takes on a very definite shape. By the time an arrangement is started we should know exactly what we want to do, leaving only the details that the flowers and leaves themselves will dictate as they are placed in position.

It is possible for floral arrangement to follow any one of the seven designs of basic art; however, in the United States it more or less falls into the design classifications of line, mass, line-mass, and circular. In other words the patterns of the triangle, the rectangle, the Hogarth curve, and the circle are more adaptable to our need.

The proposed location will influence the selection of container, style of arrangement, floral material, textures, size of units, color, and accessories (if any). Thus it is important to know where the arrangement will be placed in the home as well as where it will be staged in a flower show. Placement in a

15

show is apt to be in a bare niche with three enclosing walls. In a home, conditions are more varied. Whatever they are, they should be taken into proper account before the arrangement is planned.

Balance is one of the basic problems of design. This means, first of all, that each item (container, stand, flowers, and accessories) must be properly related to the others in size and weight—for instance, proper balance is difficult to achieve with flowers that are either too small or too large for the container chosen.

The arrangement itself can be balanced symmetrically or asymmetrically. Symmetrical balance is expressed easily and clearly with two roses of equal size and similar coloring and shape. Placing one rose on one side of an imaginary axis at a certain height and angle and repeating with a second rose on the opposite side at the same height and reverse angle demonstrates symmetry. Asymmetry has been explained as "making unsymmetrical masses appear to be of equal weight." In other words, working with unequal elements or masses, we arrange these unequally, yet so that the total effect is one of balance or equally distributed weight.

We find that the farther from the center an object is, the greater its weight or attraction. Thus, balance may be achieved by placing a large or more colorful flower near the center of the design with a smaller one farther from the axis on the opposite side. Two flowers of identical coloring and size will vary in weight projection when one is short-stemmed and placed near the center and the other, with a longer stem, is placed farther away. The second will appear to have more weight. A flower with more vivid coloring or one larger in size appears to be heavier in combination with smaller, less vivid flowers.

Since judging comments can be vague, entrants will be wise to analyze the balance of a design and to train their eyes to recognize perfection when they see it.

A pattern of intersecting triangles forms the basis of this design of five tulips in an alabaster bowl. Petals of the two lower tulips are folded back to add visual weight at the base of the arrangement.

16

18

Sometimes if we observe a landscape artist, we will see him remove his canvas from the easel, hold it upside down, and perhaps even swing it. He may step away several paces in various directions. Why? He is checking the balance of this composition on his canvas. While we cannot, of course, turn an arrangement upside down, we can do one of several other things. First of all, we can study our arrangement in a mirror. This is like having an extra eye, or at least a fresh eye, with which to look critically at our work. We can also help train our eyes by making a pencil drawing (it need not be perfect) of the principal lines of an arrangement, to see if the continuation of a line here or the shortening of a line there would improve the composition and bring it into better balance. We can see if the main line curves too far right or left, giving a feeling either of backache or of something falling on its nose. We can check the size of the leaf units, and study the placing of the focal point. Is there enough weight at this or that point, or would a slightly altered position balance the design better? Drawings can help us determine many things about a design.

Not long ago I judged an arrangement which used several flowers of one type, all of identical size. The main line not only ended with a fully opened flower, but was pulled far to the right, inches over the imaginary focal-point line, thus giving an insecure look to the whole arrangement even though the material itself was well anchored in the holder. A pencil drawing might have demonstrated its lack of balance to the exhibitor.

For at-home self-examination, I frequently use a black-and-white photograph of an arrangement. I outline the dominant parts with India ink, bleaching out all details and leaving only outline. This results in a lesson of enormous value.

Another way of seeing a design with new eyes is to use binoculars, looking at it through one end and then the other. Yet another simple check is to use a square of blue glass to eliminate the distraction of color and permit you to evaluate the directional lines only.

Tendrils of a wild vine and branches of *Euphorbia polychroma* form the curve of this arrangement. A stick wedged in the vase holds stems in place.

If you are lucky enough to own a Polaroid Land camera, you can photograph an arrangement and have a print of it a minute later. This is always a useful check. A black-and-white picture will show pattern clearly, for the intoxicating effect of color will have been removed. You can study the picture from all angles and, like a painter, check to see how the composition looks upside down.

The location of an arrangement must be taken into account, as in some locations balance can sometimes be quite complicated. The Japanese use the plain, wide, built-in *tokonoma* (alcove) for staging, so balance and proportion do not pose the same problem. Immediate surroundings become doubly important when an arrangement is used with furniture or as part of a table setting. The environment in any part of a room may influence a design's over-all size, causing it to vary, yet still remain in balance. A sizable picture hung in close proximity may indicate the necessity for greater height in an arrangement than we might otherwise give it. In other words, one element influences the other. Equally, in a table setting, other pertinent objects become part of the over-all design; the flower arrangement must be well balanced within itself and, at the same time, must be in proper scale with its surrounding elements.

Design has two important aspects: first, the structural; and second, the ornamental. These two factors, however, are not divorced. The structural, like the skeleton of a building, sets the shape of a design, while the ornamental is largely superimposed as we fill in with flowers and foliage to give the composition color and fullness of form. The ultimate idea is unity.

Besides the size of our floral material, color has visual weight, and this we also balance harmoniously throughout our design. An artist frequently develops his color scheme by placing small dots of paint here and there on the canvas, emphasizing one color more than another, and then using transitional colors or hues to blend and help balance the design. This process of balancing and blending colors is equally important in arranging flowers tastefully. While

Open Strelitzia (bird-of-paradise) blossoms form a rhythmic pattern above the sand-blasted driftwood set in a wooden bowl. The main stalk is an unopened Strelitzia bud. Camellia foliage fills the areas between the flowers.

20

all the flowers of one color should not be spaced out evenly to look like pins in a pincushion, neither should all the material of one color be concentrated in one part of the design at the expense of another. An exception here may be the use of a different color consolidated at the focal point.

As a rule, units of a design should be larger and stronger in color at the base and toward the central axis or center of balance, and grow smaller and lighter in hue and fewer in number toward the outline. The use of larger or brighter flowers at the top of an arrangement will usually make a design look top-heavy. Contrasts of color, such as light against dark and dark against light, can make an otherwise monotonous pattern look alive.

While we build an arrangement we must not overlook the sides and the back. Even when an arrangement is to be seen from one side only, the design must have a three-dimensional quality. Lines drawn with bare branches are beautiful but on their own usually lack depth. This quality can be injected by inserting leaves or flowers, or both, to come from behind the main line; by composing units in triangles; or by facing materials in different directions. Any and all these devices are used to round out a design and avoid the appearance of thinness. Even a line design must have the appearance of depth.

Finally there is the question of rhythm. Rhythm is the element that gives the design apparent movement. It may be in the measured, proportional intervals of flower or leaf placement, or in other repetitive forms—just so long as monotony (pat, flat patterns) is avoided. There is rhythm in the relation of parts, one dominant, another subordinate. An obvious example of rhythm is found in the placement of tree branches, or in the sweep of an "S" curve.

There is much to guide us in our designing. A study of nature should come first. If we note the way things grow in the garden, we see groupings of flowers and shapes that suggest an attractive indoor arrangement. We see branches with attractive curves, and in leaves and flowers we see patterns within patterns. Then too, if we are prepared to study nature through the eyes of others, we can learn much by visiting art museums and observing the way artists have handled their composition at juxtaposition of color. Flower and still-life paintings by the masters offer an endless study; so do books with reproductions of paintings or prints by the Europeans and the Orientals. All of this can take us far in the art of arranging flowers in beautiful designs.

Clusia leaves, Viburnum nana foliage and Irish bells in a Chinese brush bottle. White eggplants are impaled upon branches heavy enough to hold them in place. The figurine balances the composition.

23

An unusual, modified pillow-type vase (higher on the left-hand side) holds a line-mass arrangement of calla lilies. Two buds form the upper points of the triangle.

24

.

CHAPTER THREE

Projects

Is it possible, you may ask, to take up the art of flower arrangement without a sizable expenditure of money and time? To this I would answer yes. Unquestionably practice is as necessary to perfection in flower arrangement as scales are to the mastery of the piano. Yet the ability to arrange flowers well can be developed in a comparatively short time if a few well-established principles are followed. As to the expenditure of money, three flowers cost less than a dozen, yet three flowers well arranged in a container can be as charming as ten times that many, or more so.

The easiest way to learn to do anything is to put ideas into actual practice. The following projects demonstrate the principles of design discussed in the previous chapter, and by following them through you will have all the grounding you need to go on and make beautiful designs of your own.

PROJECT 1

Materials used: Nine pussy willows. Container: One cake pan. Holder: Needle point. One block of modeling clay.

The Arrangement: You may ask, "Why nine pussy willows? Why not eight or ten?" And "No flowers?" We start with three, five, seven, or nine stems because good results are more easily achieved with odd numbers when less than ten units are used. As you practice, build, rebuild, and analyze, you will discover the workability of odd numbers. Since balanced form can be observed better when distracting elements are at a minimum, no flowers have been used in this first project.

1. For any arrangement, symmetrical or asymmetrical, a holder is first selected. If a needle point holder is chosen, anchor it first with modeling clay. This can be accomplished only if the holder, container, and clay are all dry. Enough dry clay is broken from the block to spread liberally over the bottom of the holder, which is then pressed onto the floor of the container. Don't forget that if any one of the three is wet while performing this step, the clay will not hold and the first heavy stem will tip the holder over.

2. We start with the main branch—measuring it to a length of about two and a half times the diameter of the container. The stem is first out straight across, then clipped upward two or three times. Sometimes the end of the stem will also need pounding to make insertion on the points of the holder easier and more secure.

Before making the insertion the main stem shown in the first illustration was gently bent—almost double—and later released so it would take on more of a curve. You will find that bending stems or branches will be easier if they have previously been soaked in water for a few hours. Grasp the stem firmly with both hands while bending it at the point of curve with thumbs and forefingers.

The tip end of the main stem in a design like this should be directly over the holder and it may be necessary to pull this either slightly to the left or to the right. The first grouping, or close companions to the main stem, are cut at various lengths and curved to follow the same general line.

26

PROJECT 1

3. The tallest pussy willow in the group to the left is cut twice the pan diameter or four to five inches shorter than the main stem. It is bent to form an arc, curving first slightly to the left and then, close to its ending, back to the right so the end points upward. It is impaled on the holder in a position that directly touches and follows the course of the main branch for two or three inches. The other three units of different height are bent and arranged to follow the same direction.

4. In the third group to the right of the arrangement, the main stem is cut slightly shorter than the main stem in the left group. It is anchored to touch and follow the first inch or so of the previously arranged stems. The forked form of this stem was selected for weight and interest.

Variation: A symmetrical pattern, using the same cake pan and another set of five pussy willows, was chosen for the arrangement shown in the illustration below.

PROJECT 1 (VARIATION)

First the dry holder was anchored with clay. Then, after the main, or central, willow was cut to measure approximately one and a half times the diameter of the container, it was anchored in the holder to follow a more or less straight vertical line. The stems on either side were cut about three inches shorter than the first length; up about three inches from the cut they were given a fairly sharp bend. Inserted directly against the first stem, one curved stem is placed to lead to the right, the second to the left. The lower stems are shorter, each following the vertical line of insertion briefly and then curving, one to the left, and the other to the right as shown.

These two designs, one symmetrical, the other asymmetrical, represent the basic structure most flower arrangements follow. Notice how the stems are placed as if growing from the same spot in the container, and how the curving lines compliment one another and round out the design.

PROJECT 2

Material used: Euonymus vegetus, box, gladiolus Florence Nightingale, dahlia Margaret Bowyer, *Hosta* and *Bergenia (Saxifragaceae) crassifolia.* Container: White Lenox porcelain compote. Holder: Needle point. Modeling clay.

The Arrangement: For this design the material was cut early in the morning and the stems submerged (the saxifrage entirely covered) in a half pailful of cool water, where it remained for three hours. This procedure allows the stems to fill with moisture and gives the material longer life. A needle point holder was anchored with modeling clay in the floor of the vase in the same manner as described in Project 1.

1. *Euonymus* is selected for the steeple or main line, the height decided, and the branch cut straight across. The cut is then clipped upward once or twice to impale easily on the holder.

29

Three steps in making the arrangement shown opposite. See text below.

2. Three additional *Euonymus* and tall boxwood stems are cut in graduated lengths and placed on the holder to parallel the line of the first stem. The height of the arrangement at this stage is rechecked. An over-all height three times that of the vase was established for pleasing proportions in this example.

3. Three gladiolus stems with tips varying a few inches in length are anchored to fill the space between the *Euonymus* and box. (To avoid crowding, lower florets were discarded.) A spray of box, together with one saxifrage leaf, is next inserted at lower right to balance the arrangement.

4. Two dahlias form the focal point. Before cutting, the dahlias are held together and tested against the arrangement for position and height. One stem is longer than the other. The shorter dahlia is inserted facing front and closing the open space between the right hand box and the *Euonymus*. Placed where they are, the two dahlias continue the axis line indicated by the spike gladiolus and *Euonymus*. The second dahlia inserted behind the box is turned to face right, thus giving the depth.

This arrangement had to be worked out with a limited amount of material. Had more saxifrage been available, the composition would have been improved by the addition of two leaves, one inserted on the right, the other on the left side. A second, shorter saxifrage placed slightly over the one in the design, under the front dahlia, and pulled down over the vase edge (a short length of Scotch Tape applied at the back would hold it there) would give the right side of the pattern better unity. And another leaf placed on the left side below the *Hosta* and across from the dahlia would give depth and a cleaner design pattern.

PROJECT 2

PROJECT 3

Materials used: Euonymus vegetus; French lilacs (white and lavender); lavender-pink carnations; orange and pink Fantasy tulips. Container: Russian antique chalice. Holder: Needle point. Modeling clay.

The Arrangement: The container for mass patterns may take various shapes, although my preference is often the compote. It may be metal, pottery, alabaster—any of which are highly complementary to floral materials. In this study the beautiful container and its lacy filigree are brass. The filigree is further decorated with insets of browned pink and green cloisonné. Since the chalice is not waterproof, a can containing a needle point holder has been placed inside it, as shown in the first work picture.

1. The height of the container is checked and the first stem is inserted and double-checked for height. When flowers are to be brought low over the edge of the container, as in this arrangement, allowance should be made for this added depth of floral material when establishing the best height for the tallest stem. The classic rule for proportions calls for a flower height of within one and a half times the height of a vertical container. In time we arrive at a correctly proportioned design by eye alone.

2. Most of the lilac foliage is discarded before the next stems are inserted. Lilac foliage is not very interesting; too much is apt to confuse a design.

Lilac stems are set on the holder so the flower heads form triangles as shown in the second step-by-step photograph. Since lilac stems tend to bend, behind-the-scene strength is supplied here with a small piece of folded chicken wire, inserted in the vase among the stems.

3. The design is next built with twelve carnations including one bud, first placed to the left of the *Euonymus.* Working downward, other carnations are added in a rhythmic pattern in the front, at the sides, and at the back of the arrangement to give it depth.

4. Now the tulips are inserted toward the middle of the arrangement and at right. Two white lilacs, stripped of foliage, are added next. White is in-

PROJECT 3

At left are four steps in the making of the arrangement shown above. This is the same design as illustrated in color on page 33.

cluded because a design of this dark coloring and size needs an accent of light color, for which white or yellow serves best. A pattern built entirely with deep, dark shades tends to be monotonous; furthermore, the individual structure of the flowers is lost.

5. The composition is finished with three additional heads of lavender lilacs, a length of their foliage to the lower right, and an added piece of *Euonymus* toward the middle, lower left. In the final composition the flowers face both front and back so the arrangement has depth and looks attractive from all sides.

PROJECT 4

Material used: Purple plum, snapdragons with purple-pink coloring. Brown *Galax* leaves. Container: Covered tin can. Holder: Chicken wire.

The Arrangement: A container need not always be of fine porcelain, bronze, or the like. Here a tin can was covered with a nylon stocking pulled taut over, it. A few stitches held it at the bottom, where the foot was cut away. Enough of the stocking was retained at the top to tuck down inside the can. A loose ball of crumpled chicken wire keeps it in place and acts as a holder for the flowers. Besides nylon, other materials can be used in this way to transform a common tin can into an attractive container.

A branch of plum blossom forms the main line of the arrangement. When selecting a branch for this purpose, choose one with a pleasing and ready-made curve. Half the job, or more, in making an attractive line design is already done when we start with an interestingly shaped main branch or stem.

1. The plum blossom stem is held next to the container while we judge the height of the arrangement. Then the stem is cut and inserted through the chicken wire holder.

2. Snapdragons are added next, at an angle approximately following the curve of the lower part of the plum blossom stem. Snapdragon leaves deteriorate fast, so these are cut away first. Insertion of the flowers is started with the longest stem.

3. The lowest snapdragon head (front right), a clear pink, is placed low over the *Galax* leaf, where it adds lighter color to the design and completes the crescent-shaped line of the arrangement.

Snapdragons are beautiful flowers, but they do have their own ideas about pattern. We can place stems carefully in an arrangement and then, a few hours later, find they have twisted themselves around in different directions. It is best, therefore, when you plan to use snapdragons, to let them stand in deep water overnight. The arrangement can then be done after the cut stems have stopped their curling.

36

Top: Judging the correct height for the main stem.

Above: Snapdragons are grouped before insertion.

Right: The finished arrangement.

Two steps in the making of the arrangement shown opposite. See text below.

PROJECT 5

Materials used: Euonymus radicans; Lycopodium (shipped from Honolulu); Pulmonaria, Mrs. Moon; eleven white squash; a weathered length of tree root. Container: Old battery jar covered with green drapery material. Holder: Chicken wire.

The Arrangement: The green color and texture of the fabric stretched over the container combines naturally with the materials used in this arrangement.

1. Where the root of the driftwood divides, one arm goes into the container and the other stays outside to hold it firm. The upper end of the root, together with three stems of *Lycopodium* and one of *Euonymus*, forms the top half of the design. Next, two shorter pieces of *Euonymus* are added, one on either side.

2. Shorter stems of the *Lycopodium* are anchored at the far left and *Pulmonaria* leaves are placed left and right. Needed weight is thus added to the left and the descending line of the pattern is completed at lower right.

3. The squash, used as flowers, are anchored to flexible branch stems which are strong enough to hold the vegetables in position. The smaller heads of squash are placed toward the top and the heavier ones surround the driftwood, making a triangular pattern at the base.

The same design could be worked out substituting carnations or chrysanthemums for the squash.

38

PROJECT 5

PROJECT 6

Material used: Iris and *Hosta* foliage; gladiolus Pink Elegance. Container: Brown pottery bowl. Tufa rock. Holder: Needle point. Modeling clay.

The Arrangement: Symmetrical balance does not necessarily mean making one side of an arrangement exactly like the other. The results of exact copying are usually stiff and monotonous, and the natural beauty of the material is lost. In this project symmetry is achieved by an even balance of weight, while the material at the left is arranged a little differently from that at the right.

1. Leaves. The tallest iris leaf forms the main line; the other three supplement it and give needed width to the upper part of the arrangement. The iris leaves are placed together and held at the base while the tips are pulled into position to form obtuse-angled triangles. The leaves are cut at the base and impaled as a unit on the needle point holder, as shown opposite. Minor angle adjustments can then be made, if necessary. *Hosta* leaves are added at each side—a little higher at the right to balance the slightly uneven visual weight of the iris leaves. The tallest leaf is anchored at the back of the iris leaves to give additional depth to the design. Note that at no point do the *Hosta* leaves have identical stem lengths.

2. Flowers. Two gladioli are used. Each stem is radically shortened to leave only two completely opened flowers. On one branch this meant discarding the three top buds. The flower stems are set close together on the needle point holder. Note the petal markings on each of the two larger blossoms which follow the direction of the ribbing of the two lower *Hostas*. These two florets, together with the piece of highly glazed tufa rock, constitute the axis of the design.

This is a simple but rewarding arrangement—attractive, easy to make, and far from costly. With the wealth of gladioli on hand during our blooming seasons many colors are available. This was made with a crinkly-edged variety in dusty pink—a color especially satisfying in the brown pottery bowl.

1

2

PROJECT 6

3

PROJECT 7

Material used: Dried palm leaf; one *Euonymus* branch; one gladiolus; eight roses. Container: Green pottery vase with brown and gray speckled glaze. Holder: None.

The Arrangement: The design here is a symmetrical pattern of curving vertical lines. The natural axis is the lowest gladiolus floret and nearby *Euonymus* foliage. The gladiolus stem plus the three loosely placed roses on the left, balanced by the five more closely placed roses on the right in front of the palm leaf, continue the ascending line.

1. First, the palm leaf is set in the vase. The container opening is small and the palm leaf sufficiently thick to make a holder unnecessary. Lower leaves are stripped from the *Euonymus* branch, which is then cut to length and set behind the palm with its tip-end leaves directly over the mouth of the vase. A small wire is firmly anchored around the base of the palm and the ends are twisted to hold the *Euonymus* stem in an upright position.

2. The first rose, after being stripped of its thorns, is cut to length and placed so the blossom is toward the left of the arrangement. (A good way to strip a rose stem of thorns is to fold a small piece of medium sandpaper, rough sides together, and run the stem gently through it. Rose thorns are a nuisance in the lower part of a vase; furthermore, their removal allows stems to take up more water. Cacti and other thorn-covered stems can be treated in the same way.)

3. The remaining roses are placed one after another on either side of the center to form two gently curving lines of bloom. The gladiolus stem is inserted next, then short lengths of *Euonymus* are added on both sides to round out the design; one piece is pulled down slightly over the edge of the vase as a finishing touch.

The vase is handmade Iowa pottery in a grayish brown which combines well with all floral hues. The stand under it is coffee-brown, rubbed walnut. The vase is set on the base slightly to the left for better visual proportion.

1

2

3

PROJECT 7

PROJECT 8

Material used: Yellow-orange croton leaves; day-lily stems; high-bush cranberry fruits; red coleus. Design accents: Driftwood; dried palm with decided yellow overcast; sea coral fan. Container: Large antique-bronze Oriental vase. Holder: Chicken wire.

The Arrangement: The pattern line here is drawn with the length of driftwood, strengthened and closely followed by the palm.

When this sort of material is used, mechanics play a part in the pattern plans; otherwise, execution is quite impossible. Neither the sea fan (which is dry) nor croton leaves have adequate stem lengths for anchorage; but, as this tropical foliage keeps fresh-looking for many days without benefit of water, new stems can be added.

1. Short lengths of dried day-lily stems are taped individually to the back of the croton leaves and a heavier branch is attached to base of fan.

2. A piece of chicken wire twice the height of the vase is folded in half, refolded vertically, and then inserted in the neck of the vase as a holder.

3. The driftwood is inserted far enough to hold in the neck of the vase, and the sea fan is arranged behind it so the two units form a triangle.

4. Foliage is added next, following the general line taken by the driftwood and continuing this line in an "S" fashion downward at the right to implement the curving outline of the vase.

5. Red coleus and the cranberry fruits form the focal point in the center of the arrangement.

PROJECT 9

Material used: Canna and canna leaves; driftwood; dried palm, oak galls. Container: Beige pottery bottle. Holder: None.

The Arrangement: Inspiration for an arrangement may come from unusual floral material; from a container; or from a specific need, such as a modern setting.

    Neither the pottery bottle nor the curved piece of dried palm was owned when the interesting piece of driftwood was picked up. But considering its inclusive line and termination (which looks something like an enlarged, prehistorical bug), the driftwood was bound to be useful eventually. The vase was finally discovered; the palm arrived via a local florist shop; and the three became a natural combination.

    1. The line of the design is established by the driftwood and the palm individually arranged to curl out of either side of the container. The narrow neck of the vase makes a holder unnecessary.

    2. Canna leaves from the garden are added in the shape of a fan to give weight to the central part of the arrangement, the leaf at the left being adjusted so its lower edge parallels the line of the driftwood above it.

    3. The oak galls, picked up from the side of the road, were wired together in a cluster and attached to a branch which is inserted in front of the canna leaves. The canna leaf with its hard, spiky bud was put in last, at a slight angle to connect with the top of the palm leaf and to follow the general direction of the driftwood.

    The vase with its neutral beige coloring is versatile; it is attractive with many long-stemmed flowers, especially with crooked-growing gladioli.

PROJECT 10

Material used: One red and six white anthuriums; canna foliage. Container: Glass headlight. Holder: Needle point covered with weathered driftwood.

The Arrangement: Anthuriums are often called "exotic," and they are—inasmuch as they are usually flown in from Hawaii. At the point of origin, however, they are not at all uncommon. The blossoms have much to recommend them. Their texture is like patent leather; they range in size from two to twelve inches; colors are from white through orange, pink, red, part-green, and mixtures; the blossom pattern is dramatic; and the flower keeps unusually well.

1. The needle point holder is anchored with clay toward one side of the container, and two bits of driftwood, one smaller than the other, are arranged to cover it on both sides.

2. The stem of the tallest flower, which is cut to two and one-half times the width of the shallow container, is impaled on the needle point holder to face right and extend just far enough so the blossom is about centered over the container.

3. The next tallest stem, cut a little over half the length of the first, is anchored to face in an opposing direction, and a third (at right) points down to the rim of the container.

4. With the main triangular outline of the arrangement established by the first three flowers, leaves and flowers are added to extend these lines and to fill in, the red anthurium being used as a bright center of interest, quite low and partially covering the joining of the stems.

The container was found at a Toledo flower show and is as uncommon as the flowers. It is handmade from extremely heavy, crystal-like glass, the bottom being slightly convex and giving a pleasant reflection when set directly on polished wood. It is very similar to one I remember Mr. Henry Ford once gave Mrs. Ford and in which it was my privilege to make the first arrangement. I was following the same principles of design described above, and as Mr. Ford watched me he said, "Mrs. Dunlop, did you ever study engineering?"

48

"Good heavens, no!" I replied. "I can't do even the simplest mechanical thing." "Maybe so, but you are, nevertheless, applying some of the principles in constructing the design you are building. Unless I completely misunderstand, they are also necessary for your floral arrangement." Later I realized how right he was—and, in fact, how important design is in every field of endeavor.

CHAPTER FOUR

Harmony with Color

WHEN A RAINBOW APPEARS, we do not look for a color theory; we accept its beauty and we give rotation of hue little, if any, thought. In looking at a landscape, we do the same; we are content to enjoy the way nature arranges the colors of growing things, lighting them with sun here or casting them into a shadowed area over there. We see contrasts in the garden between bright-colored flowers and dark foliage; in the woods we appreciate the subtle differences of many different greens and browns which make up endless, fascinating monochromatic patterns. These things we absorb either subconsciously or unconsciously when we enjoy nature outdoors.

Consequently there can be few people who, at the time they first start arranging flowers, do not already have at least a working knowledge of color

A pottery mallard provided the color cue for this design of dried materials. Stiff gray spikes of an ocean-washed shrub, a blond branch, bittersweet tendrils and *Asparagus plumosus* combine with chestnuts, *Ceropia Patnata,* yellow yarrow, and tulip, lotus, and monk-bread pods.

and pattern. Even when dealing with man-made things—good taste in clothes or in decorating the house—we are taught the principles of color harmony and balance. True, our eyes may have to be trained to see greater subtleties; but usually by trial and error, by comparing one color against another, we see and learn which colors go well together and which ones don't and in what proportions those selected should be mixed for the effect we are striving to obtain.

I still think the best way of learning about color is less through rules or color charts than by analyzing the arrangements of color we most enjoy in pictures, or have seen in a particular spot in the garden, or have observed in the way nature paints her birds and animals. In this manner a knowledge of color comes naturally and in a very personal way.

Where a color chart can be most helpful is in suggesting planned color combinations we may never have tried our hand at before. While most people know the contrasts they can achieve by using white against red, let us say, or red against green, or yellow against mauve, it may not have occurred to them how effective the combination of colors in a limited range (analogous colors) can also be. For instance, an arrangement of all white flowers can be every bit as beautiful as a bouquet composed of many brightly colored flowers. The different tints and tones of white, cream, and perhaps beige or even pale yellow, with green foliage can provide subtle harmonies that make such an arrangement incredibly lovely. A monochromatic arrangement using all blue or all green, or flowers all of some other color, is often a requirement of a flower show class; experimenting along these lines can be most rewarding.

While the artist can squeeze different pigments onto his palette and mix them to any hue he wants, the flower arranger must accept the fact that, aside from contributing factors such as available light, the colors of the flowers she works with are set, and no amount of doctoring will change the tint or tone of the natural blossoms. The arranger carefully selects her palette from the garden or the florist, choosing flowers in the primary colors she wants while

A study in light beige and brown with green peony foliage. The antique Chinese brush bottle container and the cat figurines are in color harmony with the magnolia tripetala flowers.

54

selecting at the same time others of harmonious in-between colors or shades with which she can round out her color design.

Colors have certain qualities which can express a mood or feeling. Red, orange, and yellow are, of course, the warm colors; blue, violet, green, and white are the cool ones. To produce a rich, vibrant, and dramatic composition, shades and tones of the warm colors (with the natural green of foliage) are used. For a quiet, cool, dainty, or more feminine effect, flowers are chosen from the range of cool colors.

When one color is featured in an arrangement, a graduation of tints and tones of that color will produce effective results. Thus a certain red may be the dominant color, and in the same hue we add other, lighter flowers graduating to tints of pink and perhaps white.

Color designs are often improved by the introduction of a small amount of a complementary color.

The use of a warm or advancing color such as red may require some discretion; that is, a greater amount of its tints with a lesser amount of its full tone value would be a wise selection. As a rule, the brightest colors are reserved for accents. When the choice is a cool color like green, the opposite method is employed—a larger amount of the strongest green would be featured with light green tints used for accent.

We learn from nature that two colors are never equally matched or balanced. One color or hue is dominant, another subordinate. Thus, in arranging flowers, we emphasize one color and use a second or third in unequal amounts throughout the arrangement. If red is used in equal quantity with jade, or yellow with violet, visually the warmth of one is apt to neutralize the coolness of the other. However, this reaction is changed if the relative amount of each is varied sufficiently.

Although arrangements have been worked out using two colors in equal amounts and balancing these equally in two halves, such as a pyramid of car-

Red ranunculus and pink roses in a red alabaster vase contrast with the green of the shiny camellia leaves. The caladium leaf, pointing downward, is light pink, the *Galax* leaves brown.

nations composed of white flowers on one side and red on the other, this is against what nature teaches us. It can only be considered as a trick effect which may, in some special circumstances, be permissible, but under most conditions is certainly not to be used.

When we talk of flowers of analogous colors we mean those most closely related—red, orange red, orange, and yellow; or on the opposite side of the color wheel, green, blue green, blue, and violet. These analogous colors can provide the idea for an effective color design worked out in either range of color.

Green (which appears in nearly every flower design because foliage is the natural complement to every flower) can be an important study in itself. The various overcasts which influence the reflection of different greens is important. Just as many leaves are undistinguished in shape, so some of them lack distinctive color and texture. For both reasons, and also because many leaves don't last as well as the flowers of the same plant, we may discard them and use other, more interesting foliage in our arrangement.

The green of certain leaves goes better with some flowers than others. For instance, greens with deep tone values, such as those of evergreens, pittosporum, or camellia foliage, are particularly satisfactory with white flowers. White with green always has stunning possibilities. Nature also provides yellow-green foliage: box, jet berry, ginkgo, and leaves of other trees. Yellow-green foliage is an especially happy choice for yellow flowers. Greens strongly influenced by gray, such as we find in the leaves of mullein, *Hosta grandiflora,* eucalyptus, and artemisia, are eagerly sought after because they combine happily with either cool- or warm-colored flowers.

Another good mixer is brown, a color naturally found on the stems of plants or branches of trees. Brown can be added to an arrangement in the form of driftwood or bark; we can also use seed pods, grasses, and fall foliage. Flowers in tones of orange, many quite browned, are available to combine with fall reds, other orange values, and yellows. Other attractive browns can be found in Japanese maple, *Galax* (in the spring), and in the foliage of a true garden aristocrat—copper beach. With its brown paperlike leaves, copper beach is especially beautiful with yellow, orange, or white flowers.

White is a very useful color for staging contrasts and enlivening an arrangement. Designs, especially large ones made up of one color, can often be improved if a small quantity of clear, strong white is introduced. For instance, the mauve and purple of stock or the vividness of red carnations become more intense and striking when one or two white flowers are strategically placed in the arrangement. Similarly, a large vase of mauve lilac can become more distinctive with the addition of a few well-placed white lilac flowers. In a relatively dark corner of a room, white is a useful color to give an arrangement importance—bring it forward, so to speak—and to contribute additional cheer to the setting.

Like white, yellow is another "carrying" color, useful in projecting itself from a dark corner or across a large room. Yellow and white arrangements are sunny and fresh-looking, and they always react well under artificial light. Contrary to a lot of general thinking, red, though a warm, advancing, and vibrant color which also stands up well under artificial light, has not the same carrying power as white or yellow. However, the more yellowed a red flower may be, the farther its color will carry.

We should remember that all color is reflected light. An object has color only in relation to its ability to reflect certain kinds of light and in relation to the color of the light directed upon it. Whenever possible, therefore, flowers should be checked for color in the place they are to be seen. Their appearance will be affected not only by the direct source of light, either natural or artificial, but also by the quantity and quality of light reflected from the walls and objects near them.

To return to the color red, many arrangers will remember when it was said, "All we need do to win a blue ribbon from the male members of the jury is to make the composition in reds"! This is not quite as true as it used to be, though it is possible that men consider red to be one of their colors—as opposed, for instance, to pink. Every color does, as suggested earlier, produce an emotional effect upon the observer. Bright colors are gay; cool colors, quiet; pastel colors, dainty; and white is often associated with formality, in an event such as a wedding. Although our aim is not to become psychologists, the occasion, the audience, or guests, should be taken into proper account along with the setting when we choose colors and a theme for a party arrangement.

Texture is also part of the color story. The characteristic of a plant tissue may be fine, like a rose petal, or shiny to the point of resembling patent leather, as is the case with the anthurium. Such qualities in different flowers can be color-absorbing or color-projecting and therefore aid or hinder our purpose of color harmony. The texture of a flower as well as its color may make it more or less suited to a particular container. In combined materials, "fitness" should be an objective.

Finally there is the question of the color and texture of the background. Pure white or black may tend to overpower the colors of the plant material. For the flower show, gray or a grayed tint of some one hue usually proves the most suitable. I once made a long trip to see an expensive staging of flower arrangements which defeated its own purpose, as well as mine. The backdrop was black velvet! The texture and color of the background absorbed much of the plant coloring. Had individual spotlights illuminated each arrangement from above, the effect might have been different.

In the home we have to work with the background we have, and in this connection we favor flowers in hues that will blend or contrast with the colors already established by the room's furnishings. That is, we do as much as we can. There is great merit in arranging flowers in the position they are to occupy. Then we can judge not only the best height for an arrangement, but also its shape and the quantity of this, that, or another color we should use to produce the most pleasing design.

The housewife who wants a simple floral decoration for her living room must keep in mind that there are no bad colors, per se. Flower arrangement hues are selected as logically as those for interior decoration. Referring to the landscape we rediscover that color in simple, natural expression is apt to be the most peaceful, satisfying, and compatible. Do not allow the rules and tools of other pursuits and arts to confuse color thinking and make floral harmonies frustrating or difficult.

The white faces of the highly improbable but decorative cats contrast with the browns of their bodies, which blend into the mauve, greens, and grays of the Echeveria and the *Kalanchoe beharensis*. Contrasts in shapes and textures were also planned. The leaves at the top are cut palmetto.

A pyramid of brown-yellow corn, yellow daisy chrysanthemums, *Mahonia*, and driftwood. As with stemless fruits, corn can be wired or impaled upon sticks which will hold in position on a needle-point holder. A wedge of soft wood was driven into the base of the driftwood so that it could be pressed down firmly onto the holder.

Opposite: The straw-colored parasol makes a fitting background for the bright "Japanese print" colors of the red ranunculus, mauve and green Echeveria, and the bright turquoise alabaster container. The handle of the parasol continues the main line of the design.

63

CHAPTER FIVE

Containers

FOR SOME YEARS I have been a speaker for the public relations bureau of the large Detroit department store, J. L. Hudson Company, where many flower shows, with the local garden clubs participating, have been staged. Lecture listeners have often suggested that with all the containers in the world placed at my disposal the task of making arrangements must be greatly simplified. This is both true and not true. As arrangers know, one can really never have too many containers; but as many of them also know, a whole closet full of beautiful vases and dishes of every type will not guarantee a blue ribbon.

The collecting of well-designed vases with interesting textures and coloring becomes important with most people who go in for arranging flowers. To ac-

Two hand-carved banana-wood figurines set in front of a tray form part of this design. Branches of ginkgo are used with *Euonymus vegetus* and a cluster of red and yellow azaleas.

quire interesting containers, we must search as does the buyer for other needs as well as those of the flower arranger. Budgets being what they are, "all the containers in the world" are not always on a department store's shelves. At times, though the ones available may not be exactly what we are looking for, one or another of them might suggest a new approach to flower design. So, yielding to this challenge, we add one more container to our collection.

In the old days containers were always "vases." Today when we use the term "vase" we may mean not only a vessel possessing greater depth than width, but a bowl or dish; we may be referring to *usabatas* or *suibans* from the Orient, or perhaps to containers which hold no water at all—a tray, slab of wood, driftwood, etc., many of which, properly selected, lend themselves to floral use.

So much has already been said and written concerning shape, texture, and color suitability that one might feel containers could by now be definitely catalogued; yet a tall, shaped vase executed in bronze or pottery, for instance, might not be as suitable, texturewise, to the purpose were it repeated in clear glass. Thus many things must be taken into account.

An odd-shaped vase or bowl can be frustrating or it can be amusing, depending upon the materials we have at our disposal. By and large, however, our selections should be confined to standard containers that are known to work best for classic line arrangements or for mass or line-mass designs. Some shapes work equally well for all three. The two-piece bronze *usubata*, used so effectively by Japanese Ikebana artists in the *Ikenobo* and other schools, is an example of one that is adaptable to many designs. The Occidental potters produce a similar form in one-piece pottery or porcelain (the compote type). Executed in a neutral coloring, these containers have many uses. So do Japanese containers based on the shape of the Chinese brush bottle which are made in bronze, pewter, or pottery.

A simple line arrangement made with stems of peach blossom in a small-sized, very ancient bronze *usubata*. The stand for the container is a polished cherry root.

66

67

Generally speaking, line arrangements can be made equally well in tall or very shallow containers. Mass arrangements, depending upon the skill of the builder, are equally at home in the same vessels.

As to color for all-around use, containers with muted colorings are the most practical. Any pure hue which has been grayed down is muted or more neutral in color. The quieter the color, the less likely it is to compete with the floral material used. Subtle shades of brown and green are popular, as is a neutral gray. Copper is particularly flattering to autumn materials, and to reds, yellows, and greens. Clear crystal or glass is lovely with any colored flowers, though it is perhaps the most difficult of all material to use. Pottery in dull glazes is particularly useful and comes in many colors—and so our collection can go on and on.

When we come to a pure white container, especially one finished in a high glaze, we must remember that it will have a strong carrying quality. I have listened to a discussion of containers and heard it said that white is neutral with any hue. This is not so. White is a color and should be regarded as such when deciding whether it is suited to the flowers you want to arrange. On the other hand, I have heard people say only white flowers can be used in a white vase. This is not true either. Certainly white flowers look lovely in a white container, but so does a mixture of other colors including white. We have only to visit shows and see the many beautiful, colorful creations built around a white vase and suffering no loss of face thereby.

The texture of a container is also of significance. Bronze, which is not always easy to come by, is a case in point. This metal is indeed versatile. Fresh branches, foliage, and most flowers are adaptable; although, in my opinion, dried materials very frequently are not. The difference in texture between a highly polished container and dried material is not always pleasing.

An antique alabaster vase of particularly attractive shape and proportion holds a symmetrical mass arrangement of yellow-tinted and honey-colored carnations, yellow roses, and tulips. Tightly closed white lilac buds, fuchsia, *Galax*, *Lycopodium* (Honolulu), *Euonymus vegetus,* and gladiolus complete the design.

I have always felt that combining silver hollow ware (much as I love it) and formal materials poses a texture problem. There is a quality of hardness in silver which stands out, perhaps due to the high polish generally used. The long-ago rule, "roses always in silver," has lately been subjected to much re-evaluation. It may be largely a question of taste here, because while many people have arrangements in silver, I personally would rather use other metals —bronze, copper, pewter—all or any of which make for warmer, subtler reflections and, I think, a happier marriage of textures.

Glass containers may be thin and fragile or thick and solid. Not only are texture, weight, and transparency or opacity of glass important in its contributing effect upon an arrangement, but so, too, are the shape and color of each piece. Sometimes antique shops can be rewarding when we look for glass. Should Lady Luck be in a liberal mood, there could be an overlay glass vase or lamp. Stem placement will not be a problem in these opaque containers and most floral textures will be found to be completely at home in them.

The texture of pottery, which may be rough or smooth, dull or highly glazed, requires equal scrutiny. Porcelain is harder and stronger than pottery, with which it is often confused, but it is much thinner and smoother; its translucency and the bell-like tone produced when it is tapped with a fingernail make it seem as light and delicate as blown glass. Its uses are more refined and formal than those of pottery and the heavier, rustic stoneware.

When selecting a "wardrobe" of vases, the astute student exercises the same judgment of texture and suitability as in selecting clothes. Placing an informal arrangement of wildflowers, driftwood, and stones in a porcelain compote would be as illogical as wearing walking shoes with an evening gown. In time, the accumulation of bowls, pots, vases, and jugs may become so considerable that more than one container of the right size, shape, color, and style will be available; in this case texture becomes the deciding factor in making a choice for a specific purpose.

An interestingly textured driftwood container in which a tin of water is concealed holds gay branches of *Magnolia Soulangeana*. A large, fully opened flower is inserted to form the focal point.

70

71

An old fruit can was soldered to the top of a blue glass oil lamp to make this unusual container. Arranged are a collection of spring flowers, predominantly blue, including hyacinth, grape hyacinth, and iris. Yellow primulas highlight the design.

Opposite: A pair of Japanese pottery wall vases. These containers are purposely not hung in a straight line. The arrangements follow a Hogarth pattern with the line starting at the upper left leaf, continuing down through the two flowers, the heads of each figurine, over the basket, and ending in a long sweep of "monkey tail."

Besides artistic suitability there is also the very practical question of whether or not a container is completely watertight. It is well to test for leakage before use. Pottery may be porous; metal seams may not be completely welded. Pottery leakage can sometimes be corrected by flushing a layer of melted paraffin over the inside; metal usually needs additional soldering. Alabaster enjoys a well-deserved popularity, but water and plant material may destroy the glaze or the color; may even cause the vessel to disintegrate. This once happened to a favorite of mine. It had not only been filled with water but immersed in it as well, to keep the flowers fresh overnight. The floral material kept, but my lovely compote did not. Ancient alabaster was a form of marble, but modern alabaster may be badly affected by water. To be

This Japanese basket, originally designed for knitting needles, is equally adaptable to flowers. A glass was inserted in the basket to hold water. Peeled driftwood, *Mahonia*, red flowering eucalyptus pods, and a cluster of spruce cones are arranged in it with a fan.

Opposite: A basket in soft muted coloring makes an attractive container for a roadside vine and the blossoms of *Magnolia Soulangeana*. As in the illustration at left, the basket contains a can of water in which the stems of the flowers are inserted.

sure of preserving it, fill the container with clear sealer (available at hardware stores) and let it stand for two or three hours, then pour the sealer back into the can and let the alabaster container dry from twenty-four to thirty-six hours.

Favorite containers that do leak or cannot be filled with water can often be made serviceable by inserting a tin can or bowl inside them which will hold the water and remain out of sight. This device is also used with arrangements made in driftwood or in baskets. Should the top of this inner container show, it can usually be covered by foliage brought down low over its edge.

Whatever you do when selecting a vase, be sure not to select one with a fancy or ornate pattern; those decorated in flamboyant colors should be avoided like the plague.

A modern replica of an old Japanese bamboo vase contains oriental poppies and foliage. The flowers were cut and treated as recommended in notes on the care of flowers given at the end of the book. They remained as arranged for five days without deterioration.

Opposite: A miniature arrangement composed entirely of beet tops in a bronze chalice. The background, which houses a netsuke, is an up-ended Chinese pottery dish, rose colored and with a crackle finish.

76

This porcelain compote comes from Italy. It looks costly but is in reality quite inexpensive. It makes an effective centerpiece, and the all-around decoration can be looked under by guests seated on opposite sides of the table. The floral material used is Jan De Graff's Enchantment lily and Viburnum nana.

Opposite: A white porcelain basket makes a fitting container for two stems of geraniums. These are held in place by a needle point holder. Nothing could look more natural or effective than this type of Ikebana, yet it is easy to do.

Two antique Chinese pottery vases of light beige coloring are used side by side for a single design of calla lilies, leaves, *Philodendron giganteum*, and *Dieffenbachia picta*.

A pair of modern glass vases of red-brown color are used for this two-in-one composition. One vase was placed on a black glass stand, giving irregularity of height. The red-flecked Haslerova dahlias and the *Mahonia* foliage are arranged to continue the sweeping lines of the cornucopia forms.

CHAPTER SIX

Rules, Shows, and Judging

WERE IT POSSIBLE to provide a few magic rules stating the exact number of flowers to be used, of prescribed height, color, forms, and combination, it would, I suppose, provide a panacea that would standardize floral arrangements. Presumably the author of such rules would be able to foretell all plant performance and insure the perfection of any design. The student would be relieved of all worries beyond finding the prescribed flowers and learning a few mechanics. Not a very creative idea, perhaps, but a safe one. True, you might long to fetch the last two lovely roses into the house before the frost— but not if the rules say "no."

Two beautiful "green jade" parrots made of fake alabaster form the focal point of this line-mass design of Strelitzia blossoms, cut-leaf philodendron, and small pineapples.

Just as a garden does not grow according to any man-made laws, rigid rules will not make perfect flower aramgements. I stress this simply because many people have been so frightened by misguided talk of "rules" that they insist they can't do arrangements. This is a pity; actually, anyone who can sew a fair seam, knit a well-fitting sweater, and arrange household effects attractively must certainly have sufficiently skillful hands and enough of an innate sense of balance and proportion to master the fundamentals of flower arrangement. Rules may help us while we are learning about designs and color, but later an attempt to follow them slavishly is more likely to close, rather than open, the door to inspiration and beauty. Besides, flower arranging is meant to be fun. If we think of principles rather than rules it *can* be fun and, at the same time, more interesting arrangements are likely to result.

While limitations are necessary in certain set situations, they are not pertinent to artistic creation. In table setting, for instance, custom, tradition, and practicality determine the placement of china and silver. Common sense dictates that flower decorations should not be so overpowering that they dwarf enjoyment of the meal, nor so large that the guests cannot see one another! Apart from these limitations, only the basic principles demonstrated in Chapter 3 need be the guide. The actual question of the kind and colors of flowers to be used, the style and shape of the container, must be decided by the individual in relation to the occasion, the time of day, the furnishings of the room and table, the lighting, and individual preferences and taste. There is no arbitrary "right" or "wrong" in such a situation. We have to do what seems most natural and suitable with available material.

I have had some sad experiences with people who felt there was a set of absolutes which could and must be followed. Not long ago, in a Michigan town, I set up a demonstration design showing a certain color progression and included the only two flowers of a particular hue that were available. As I finished, one lady jumped to her feet saying, "You can't show that—it's all

Pottery parakeets accent the exciting tropical coloring of *Anthurium Scherzerianum* and contrast with the deeper green of the *Euonymus radicans*. Flowers and leaves follow and soften the vertical line of the weathered driftwood.

wrong. You have used only *two* tulips!" She had completely overlooked the fact that there were other blossoms, equally important, which balanced the design and did, as a matter of fact, bring the unit count to an odd number. Although one must concede that odd numbers have a certain magic significance in an arrangement, this is not to say that every flower must be exactly counted before we make an arrangement. Our eyes will tell us better whether we have put in one too few or one too many.

There is one situation for which unbreakable rules are provided and must be followed. The arranger who has progressed to entering creations in flower shows and competitive exhibitions will find they are governed by a list of requirements which *must* be met. Such requirements are not necessarily a guide to esthetics; frequently they are set to test the skill of the contestants. Flower show rules also represent a basic standard of comparison by which entries may be classified and judged. These rules are printed in the schedule adopted for each show. Many groups will follow standard schedules suggested by state or national garden groups. While these serve an excellent, practical purpose in organizing a show, they are not meant to be endlessly transferable from the exhibition hall to the home, where a quite different set of circumstances may exist.

In a competition, however wise or, perhaps, foolish the rules are, they must be followed to the letter. When a class calls for roses, use roses; if you don't want to, then change classes or don't exhibit. If red roses are indicated, check the color in both daylight and artificial light. If a height hazard is included, measure meticulously to an eighth of an inch. If there is a "passing committee," get the sanction of not one, but all the members. While there is every reason to comply exactly with the announced regulations of any competition, neither the jury nor the entrant should go beyond the schedule, making up new rules or adding old ones.

There was a day when every floral design had to be measured to the exact inch and every judge sallied forth with a yardstick, using it as a badge of competence. Many are the silver bowls permanently disfigured by modeling clay (when a copper or pottery one might have been used) simply because of an unwritten "rule" which said "silver only" for roses. Nor could live flowers and leaves be used with dried leaves, or wild flowers with cultivated ones—or so it was said. Yet this happens continually in the garden. We think of Queen Anne's lace or dandelions as "wild" and of clematis as "tame," but such distinctions should not exist in art any more than they do in nature. At home, use what you want where you want and be guided only by what you see will be suitable and pretty in the setting. But when exhibiting, be sure to check the amount of latitude allowed by the rules of the particular class you are entering. Sometimes they limit types of material, sometimes they don't. In actual fact, the greater the limitation the more challenge it represents, the more ingenuity you are called upon to display, and the more you learn about flower arranging as a consequence.

When we have an open mind, there is always much to be learned at every flower show. Some exhibitors may have used branches or horticultural specimens we have never thought of using ourselves, and thus new plant acquaintances are made. The neighbor in the next niche may use different mechanical devices or demonstrate a quite new way of expressing pattern or an idea. Wherever we look, we can learn something about materials, color, design; we can learn from well-arranged exhibits as well as from those that display obvious weaknesses.

In shows where judging is not comprehensive, the entrant may learn much by listening to visitors. Their down-to-earth comments are often quite analytic and useful, even if sometimes deflating to an exhibitor whose arrangement may be analyzed within her hearing.

Sometimes a criticism may be well made, at other times of course it may not be, even by a judge. At this time there is no substitute for a sense of humor. One lady I know who had studied six years in Japan came home, entered the "Oriental" class at a show, and found her entry was disqualified as "not Japanese"! I have also seen a three-hundred-year-old pewter and silver tea caddy

An old Japanese bronze moon container is filled with a crescent of daffodils and *Juniperus excelsa stricta*. The evergreen combines well with other flowers and can remain in place when fresh blossoms are needed to replace the old ones.

Opposite: Two Chinese brick-shaped vases, one arranged diagonally over the other on a polished board. They hold two branches of flowering peach and a mass of *Helleborus* (Christmas rose). The tallest branch is anchored to a well-secured needle point holder in the lower vase; the one at right spreads out from the upper vase. Christmas roses are arranged in both of them.

Right: A sweeping "S" shape or Hogarth curve is worked out here with *Euonymus kewensis*. Blossoms of clematis Ville de Lyon are used at the center. The arrangement in a bronze vase on a teak stand is staged on a tall, well polished cherry root.

described on a score card as "tin" and authentic old Celadon plates pegged as "cheap ironstone." The fact is, some judges may be strong on some points but weak on others; some of them know antiques, others actually pride themselves on *not* knowing them.

Those connected with teaching or demonstrating flower arranging, even students and their families, must often listen to complaints concerning flower show judging results. At times these complaints have been justified. To meet this problem, the New York Federation of Garden Clubs originated courses of specialized training for judging horticulture and flower arrangements as well as flower show practice. Women from all over the country attended these classes. Later, under the leadership of Mrs. Jerome W. Coombs, then the national chairman, courses were organized for a wider audience in the judging schools of the National Council of Garden Clubs.

It is well to remember that students of Ikebana in Japan study for years before being certified as "masters," but a judging school graduate in the United States may receive her certificate after a very brief period of study. Then too, not everyone has the same perception, the same understanding of design or appreciation of color values. Arrangements may include antiques, porcelain, china, crystal, linens, silver, or accessories of many types; and it takes more than a few easy lessons to learn to judge the appropriateness of such objects and their affinity with the flowers selected for a particular setting or situation.

Unhappiness may stem not only from a jury's lack of experience, but also from the compromise decisions which take place. It has long been my private theory that one well-versed judge is more helpful for the entrant and the public than three with varied opinions and backgrounds.

The circle is one of art's basic designs. Here the continuous line is broken with flowers and foliage at the base and top. The wheel is nailed to a small board on which a needle point cup holder is also placed. Gladiolus Bonnie Prince and *Euonymus vegetus* make a beautiful combination.

The cock and hen in this table decor are made of glittering brass. The tail feathers of the hen set the pattern for the arrangement of the flowers (*Clethra Anifolia rosea*) and the slender yellow ears of Iowa corn. A small cup container is entirely covered by foliage.

Cycas, gladiolus, and yellow daffodils arranged on a driftwood
stand with terra-cotta geese. Brown tumblers, place mats, teak-
handled flatware and wooden plates are used with red-orange
napkins and a green glass serving dish.

95

Rhythm is emphasized in this arrangement of desert spoon (*Dasylirion Wheeleri* root) and lemons which combine handsomely with *Lycopodium* and dried palm in the tall pottery vase.

Opposite: A curving triangular arrangement of *Hosta* leaves and mandrake (May apple) flowers in a shallow pottery container. The leaves of the mandrake were cut away. Tufa rock covers the needle point holder.

Having decisions announced over a public address system is also an excellent idea. Errors of judgment may occur, but honest mistakes frankly acknowledged are usually accepted graciously. Both exhibitor and audience can learn much from oral judging, which, when properly handled, also raises the show standard. Oral judgments have to be complete and explicit, with no chance for favoritism. Naturally exhibitors are disappointed when they do not

96

Sleek heads of Strelitzia blossoms emerge from their own foliage in this striking arrangement in a light brown pottery vase. Stiff, bristling palm sheaths are wired together at the base.

Opposite: Dried *Hosta* leaves and okra pods surround a hand-carved banana-wood figurine. The leaves were dried by placing the stems in a container with a short supply of water which was allowed to evaporate.

100

The debris of an early Michigan mine yielded the beautiful pieces of Keweenaw County "Irish leaf" copper featured in this arrangement. Chrysanthemums and prickly pear accent the rich copper tone of the tallest piece; two Mexican peppers reflect the unusual deep amethyst coloring of the heavier piece, which conceals the needle point holder. *Mahonia* leaves help to round out the design.

A line-mass arrangement of *Rhus Cotinus* (smoke tree), fall foliage, and red and orange blossoms of gladiolus Wonder Boy and Traveler. Seed pods of pokeberry and one pod of *Arisaema triphyllum* (jack-in-the-pulpit) enter the design at the lower right and hang gracefully over the edge of the container.

A natural bamboo stalk container is arranged here with Scotch pine and a focal point of geraniums. The evergreen was trimmed to give an upward sweep of line. A needle point holder was used in the waterproof can which lines the container.

Five sansevieria spikes and two poinsettias form a simple, dramatic pattern. The lowest spike was Scotch-Taped in a curve for twenty-four hours before the design was made. Orchid tubes provide moisture for the poinsettias. The sansevieria is kept dry.

This modern version of the Japanese container is a magnet for spring-flowering branches. The selection consists of two magnolia stems, the longer one with interesting curves sweeping far to the right.

Opposite: This branch of a thorn tree was forced into flower indoors where it remained in blossom for two weeks. The end of its stem was pounded and clipped upward several times until it held firmly on the needle holder, which was heavily anchored with clay. An open camellia flower, bud, and foliage form the focal point.

The bronze *usubata* and stand are the only truly Japanese components in this study. However, the five unfolding leaves of the brown canna are bent and manipulated to follow more or less the classical lines represented by the Japanese method of flower arrangement.

110

This pyramid, composed of miniature pineapples, three artichokes, a pomegranate, and Ti and pandanus foliage, was used on a coffee table at Thanksgiving. The driftwood is self-supporting. A tin container, concealed in the wood, holds the upper leaves and fruit; another one is concealed by the material at the base.

Four *Clematis Henryi* flowers are backed with pointed lupine leaves, one for each flower. The clematis bud is added for variety of form. Two day-lily leaves give the arrangement the height needed for the tall container.

CHAPTER SEVEN

Cut Flower Treatment

HOW A FLOWER IS TREATED from the time it is cut until it is placed in an arrangement is important to its length of life. All flowers do not have the same fiber construction or, therefore, the same basic keeping qualities. However, if these differences are taken into consideration from the time stems are cut, the life span of many of them can be lengthened. One thing at the start—be sure to use a very sharp knife or a pair of sharp scissors so you can make a clean, sharp cut.

The basic constructions of plant stems fall into six general classifications: bulbous, woody stem, hollow stem, annuals, those requiring no water, and milky sap stems.

Bulbous Flowers. Common examples in the bulbous category are tulips, lilies, and gladioli. When gathering tulips in the garden I carry a pail with enough water so the ends of their stems can immediately be covered as I cut them. Indoors I wrap a bundle of the tulips up in a sheet of newspaper, with the blossoms showing over the edge. The paper is tight enough to keep the stems straight. I then submerge the package, up to the flower heads, in a laundry tub of water, where it stays until I am ready to use the tulips. I do the same with lilies, with one difference. Once I have cut enough lilies for my purpose I separate them and wrap them in groups of three to protect the fragile petals, then each grouping is placed loosely in a fruit-juice can of water for hardening before use. Gladioli are not wrapped with paper but are placed in deep water, up to the first open flower.

Woody Stems. These materials comprise the flowering shrub and tree families and such flowers as stock and chrysanthemum, which usually take up water slowly. To expedite absorption, the cut ends are pounded with a mallet until the fiber is broken down. Lilacs and stock, to mention two popular flowers, will rarely last long without such treatment.

Hollow Stem. Flowers such as delphiniums and dahlias have hollow stems. They should have the blossom section protected with a sheet of tissue paper while the stem ends are submerged up to five or six inches in boiling water for at least a minute, after which they are plunged in cold water and allowed to remain there for several hours or overnight.

Annuals. Zinnias, marigolds, petunias, etc., require immediate submersion in deep water. Place them in a pail of water and leave them in a cool place for several hours before starting an arrangement.

Flowers Which Require No Water. In this classification we find the hibiscus. It lasts one day only—either in or out of water. Its short life makes its use inadvisable except, let's say, for a special party. Camellias and orchids are said to need no water; however, the individual stems can be placed in orchid tubes, and I think this makes a difference in keeping them fresh. A light, daily syringing of water on the blossoms will lengthen their life.

Asymmetrically balanced arrangement using a twirl of driftwood, a bare branch, and dahlias. The large leaf curving down over the center of the pottery vase gives the floral arrangement the illusion of greater height. Without this, the container would appear disproportionately tall.

114

A mass of white gladiolus in a white alabaster bowl. Many of the heavier individual flowers at the lower sections of the stems were discarded. In lieu of foliage, manna pods were used for line indication and color contrast.

Opposite: An apple branch, lilac blossoms, and tulips arranged in a *suiban*. In Japan, the pattern here would be classified as being in the "abstract style." It departs radically from the general rule as to the height of material in relation to the container, yet the grouping is effective.

116

Milky Sap. Stems like those of poinsettias and poppies need special treatment if they are to last any time at all. For a poppy arrangement, cut buds and allow them to open later. Carry a candle to the garden and light it while cutting. As each stem is snipped, place it quickly over the flame until it is calloused over, then place the poppy in the pail of water. If for any reason the stem length must be changed, the cut should again be scabbed over. Poinsettias should receive the same treatment. If "bleeding" is stopped before they are placed in water for a hardening period, these flowers remain in excellent condition for from five to seven days.

Almost any arrangement designed for the home will last longer if it is put in a cool place at night. The flowers will also keep longer if they are not subjected to a strong breeze. Strong winds and currents of air in the house or garden are one of the worst enemies of flowers.

OTHER MATERIALS

Clematis, which we grow in profusion, have woody stems, yet none of the above methods of preserving works a hundred per cent. The stems should be placed in water immediately; but more flowers than are needed should be cut, for invariably a few fold up.

Many foliage plants are crisper and last longest after they have been completely covered and left to stand in water. Cyclamen, lupine, *Pulmonaria,* and saxifrage leaves are examples.

Evergreens preferably are cut far in advance of arrangement. If left on the basement floor for twenty-four hours or so before use, they will wilt a little and become easier to bend into desired shapes. Stems may be bent and wired into different shapes and then submerged in water for a day to perk them up before the wire is released and the arrangement is made.

Early in the morning is the best time for cutting flowers. Evening is also good, but some varieties close for the night and may be found asleep if cut too late.

118

REVIVING TIRED FLOWERS

In the case of flowers which have been out of water too long, a shock treatment will sometimes revive them. Two vessels of water are prepared, one boiling, the other ice-cold. First, protect the blossoms from steam with a layer of paper; then recut the stem ends and plunge them into hot water until they show signs of activity (perhaps three to five minutes). Remove them and quickly submerge them in the iced water. The shock will often return them to a usable condition.

DRIED FLOWERS

Designs made with dried materials often stay around overlong. When bittersweet and many other seed pods become dusty they can be dipped in hot water to remove the soil. Incidentally, the stem of the bittersweet will become more pliant and can be rearranged after dipping in hot water.

The secret of drying flowers is to cut them at the height of their color and dry them in a dark dry place like an attic.

CONTAINERS

All containers should be completely clean before flowers are arranged in them. Bacteria left from former usage reactivates and may cause the new floral material to deteriorate.

Leaves on stems that will go down inside the vase and which are to play no part in the design should first be removed. They tend to decay and cause the flowers to die more quickly.

CPSIA information can be obtained at www.ICGtesting.com
Printed in the USA
LVOW050946300113

P7361500001B/4/P